u've Decided To

omeschool,

ow
hat?

Legal Issues

Events Calendar

Curriculum

Resources

You've Decided To Homeschool,

Now What?

Marsha Hubler

Educator, Author, Speaker, Mother

Master Books
A Division of New Leaf Publishing Group

БЯ   10.99 11/07

First printing: September 2007

ISBN-13: 978-0-89051-512-9
ISBN-10: 0-89051-512-3
Library of Congress Number: 2007925418

Cover design by Janell Robertson.

Printed in the United States of America.

Please visit our website for other great titles:
www.masterbooks.net

For information regarding author interviews, please contact the publicity department at (870) 438-5288.

Master Books
A Division of New Leaf Publishing Group

Contents

Introduction

A Challenge to Parents

The society in which we live today is a hectic one with demands that can shake the "average" American family apart at the seams or have it in a constant state of chaos. Financial pressures alone often force both parents to work, thus shortchanging the quality time that parents want and need to have with their children in the home.

Therefore, the decision to homeschool in a society such as ours is a serious one that every member of the family needs to consider. Homeschooling on the parents' part requires setting priorities that the average person sees as strange, ridiculously demanding, or at best, frivolous. Children who homeschool must learn in an atmosphere different from any other "school" they have ever attended. Yet, increasingly more parents, Christian and non-Christian, are coming to the conclusion that homeschooling might be what their children need to succeed academically in the demanding world in which we live.

In addition to the concern for academic excellence, many Christian families believe that God has delegated to them the authority and responsibility to teach their children. Christian parents who hold this conviction believe that teaching their children at home is a mandate from God, not a choice. They hold to Bible verses such as the following, which they feel clearly dictate what the parent/child relationship should be:

1. "And thou shalt love the Lord thy God with all thine heart, and with all thy soul, and with all thy might. And these words, which I command thee this day, shall be in thine heart: And thou shalt teach them diligently unto thy children, and shalt talk of them when thou sittest in thine house, and when thou

walkest by the way, and when thou liest down, and when thou risest up" (Deut. 6:5–7; KJV).

2. "Lo, children are an heritage of the LORD, and the fruit of the womb is his reward. As arrows are in the hand of a mighty man; so are children of the youth" (Ps. 127: 3-4; KJV).

3. "And ye fathers, provoke not your children to wrath, but bring them up in the nurture and admonition of the Lord" (Eph. 6:4; KJV).

Perhaps you are a Christian parent who is considering homeschooling your child because you see needs in the child's life that only an education at home can address. However, a parent who makes the decision to homeschool must come to terms with the demands of this unique academic approach. The decision to homeschool is a life-changing one for every single member of the family.

The first question you need to answer is your reason for wanting to homeschool. Homeschooling because you are angry at your public school system or because your child doesn't like the teacher(s) is often the wrong motive. Also, your decision to homeschool because your neighbor or relative does is no reason to take such a big step, or risk, with your child's academic future. Without a strong resolve based on a strong faith in God, your desire to homeschool will wane as such a weak reason fades into the sunset as the weeks and months roll by.

Skeptics ask why any parent would choose to invest so much time, and possibly hundreds of dollars each year, in a homeschool program when public education is free. And what happens, they say, to the resolve of that homeschooling family if, by the end of October, every member of the family has decided that homeschooling really isn't that much fun and that Junior should pack his Twinkies in his backpack and pile into the school bus again? Is homeschooling really such a good idea?

Homeschooling, following the proper and tested procedures, is a rewarding experience that develops well-rounded and happy children. Parents find their children bond with them and other siblings in a way that usually doesn't occur when the children attend school outside the home. With the parents' daily reinforcement of biblical principles, morals, and ideals, the children, including teenagers, develop their own set of values that are in complete agreement with what the parents believe.

Every year, over a million and a half children are homeschooled in this country by parents who have strong convictions to have complete control over what their children learn.[1] Those parents are committed "educators," teaching their children with firm resolve, even on bad days when Fido *has* eaten the homework or Junior says he hates everything, sticks out his tongue, and locks himself in the bathroom for three hours. And when the bad days seem to outnumber the good ones, those parents who have made a firm commitment to homeschool do not quit. Long before the first page of the first book has ever been opened on the first day of school, they have made a "no turning back" decision to homeschool, and to do it legally and effectively. They strive for excellence and they achieve it!

But what about you? Do you see the need to homeschool? Do your children want to homeschool? Only you and your family can answer these questions.

To help you decide if homeschooling is for you, this preface poses a short list of thought-provoking questions to consider. As you evaluate the pros and cons of homeschooling, the following questions may help you make one of the most important decisions you and your family have ever made:

1. Do I believe that God wants me to homeschool my children?
2. How concerned am I about the academic welfare of my child?
3. Do I have a determination that will weather those bad days when I can't see anything happening in my child's life except frustration?
4. Do I have the financial means to provide a good homeschool program?
5. What are my reasons for wanting to homeschool?
6. Do my children want to homeschool? Why? Why not?

If none of these questions have previously crossed your mind, an open family forum to discuss the answers would shed great light on your family's opinion of homeschooling. What every family also needs is a list of the reasons why homeschooling is a good idea.

Following is a short list of reasons why the majority of homeschooling families have decided to educate their children at home. As you analyze the list and decide to homeschool, you and your child(ren) may choose to sign on the dotted line of the "Family Commitment to Homeschool" on page 14, thus sealing the commitment to each other to tackle the enormous academic challenge that lies before you:

1. _____ I have religious convictions contrary to the philosophy of the schools.
2. _____ I believe that the schools do not have high standards of academics, discipline, or morality.
3. _____ My child has special needs that the schools cannot address (advanced learner or struggling student).
4. _____ I believe that homeschooling affords the best educational venue to meet my child's academic needs and develop his/her character to become a responsible Christian adult and a contributing member of society.

****

OUR FAMILY COMMITMENT TO HOMESCHOOL

We, _____

_____

_____

_____

_____

are committed to homeschooling. We firmly believe it is the best academic program available for our family. We will **not** quit.

Date: _____

****

Congratulations! You and your family have made the first and most important decision concerning homeschooling. You *have* decided to do it.

But I'm sure, as you evaluate the major step you are about to take, you are already asking, "What do I do now?"

The book in your hands will answer that question. In its streamlined format, the manual presents a step-by-step approach to help you organize and administrate the best homeschool program available for your child(ren) today.

I suggest that you work through the following pages in the order in which they are presented. Then complete each objective and record the date when you complete each task. When you have worked your way through the entire manual, you will have organized and administered a legal and effective full year of homeschooling, one of which your entire family will be proud.

So turn the page. You are about to launch your family into the academic adventure of a lifetime that every member will enjoy and cherish. Let's get going!

Endnotes
 1. Home School Legal Defense Association. www.hslda.org.

Chapter 1:

As You Consider Homeschooling

Since 1990, I have worked with hundreds of homeschooling families as a consultant and evaluator in the state of Pennsylvania. The overwhelming majority of families I've observed have done an excellent job teaching their children at home, most of them seeking advice from other homeschoolers, from a consultant, or from "how-to" books before they started their home education program. Successful families took the time to find out what to do, and they did it well.

However, occasionally I have evaluated a family at the end of the year (Pennsylvania state requirement) whose academic program was a disaster. In questioning the parents about the lack of progress or total disorganization in their program, I've always heard the same answer, "We didn't know what to do."

So, what should they have done?

Wise is the parent who seeks counsel as the decision is made to take this gigantic academic step. Wise is the parent who learns what his state requirements are and then explores the curriculum possibilities to provide the best academic program for his child within the boundaries of the law. Wise is the parent who visits local homeschooling families and finds out the pros and cons of "school at home" before he ever buys his first homeschooling textbook.

But where does a seeking family find this help?

To help families not only start homeschooling, but also to continue to do so effectively and legally in subsequent years, I've compiled a list of essential tasks that any homeschooling family should complete to help their homeschooling program succeed. In my years of experience, I have found that the families that had conducted ineffective homeschooling programs always pleaded ignorance, which certainly is no excuse.

As you work your way through each section of this book, your commitment to homeschool should become stronger upon completion of each task. You should also feel confident enough to remove any doubt, skepticism, and fears of failure you might have had to this point. Therefore, as you and your family set your sights on a year of homeschooling, be assured that success is on the way!

Tasks To Complete during the Year before You Start To Homeschool

(Record the date after completion)
(Date completed)

1. _____Talk to at least two homeschooling families in your area and discuss the advantages and disadvantages of homeschooling. (If you don't know any homeschoolers, post signs at libraries, convenience stores, and book stores requesting homeschooling families to contact you.)

Homeschool family's name, address, phone number, e-mail

_____

_____

_____

2. _____ Find out from new homeschooling contacts if there is a homeschool support group in your area and attend at least one meeting. Homeschool support groups meet regularly. Parents share joys and frustrations while the children engage in field trips, sports events, and extra-curricular activities such as art, music, science labs, and creative writing. Providing social interaction, competition, and just plain fun with others, support groups are a *vital* part of a well-rounded homeschool program. (See Chapter 5 that explains how to start one.)

Homeschool Support Group _____

Contact Person_____

Phone Number_____

E-mail _____

3. _____ If your state requires a homeschool evaluator, obtain information from your homeschool support group about evaluators in your immediate area. Choose one who will work with you and your family.

Homeschool Evaluator's Name_____

Address_____

_____

Phone Number_____

E-mail _____

Fee Charged Per Evaluation _____

4. _____ Attend a homeschool convention or curriculum fair to study available curricula, to meet other homeschoolers, and to attend homeschool workshops. (To find if your state has homeschool conventions, go to www.thehomeschoolmom.com.)

Name and Address of Convention _____

_____

_____

_____

Contact Person_____

Phone Number_____

E-mail _____

Website _____

Date of convention_____

5. _____ Go online to www.homeschooling. about.com and the Home School Legal Defense Association at www.hslda.org/ph. (540) 338-2733 and check your state's requirements to start a homeschooling program. (All states vary in their requirements. Some states have no requirements at all.) Print the requirements and keep them in the back of this book.

6. _____ Obtain from your school district homeschool coordinator the local homeschool requirements, if any. (School districts vary in minor issues, i.e., type of daily attendance record required, complexity of portfolio required.) Staple in back with state requirements.

Name of school district _____

Phone Number_____

Homeschool Official at That School_____

_____

Extension Number_____

E-mail _____

Example: Pennsylvania State Homeschooling Requirements

A. By August 1 of each year:
  1. Parent must register with a notarized affidavit provided by the school district or local homeschool

consultant for all children eight years or older with the local school district in which the homeschool family resides, notifying the homeschool official of the parents' intent to homeschool. The affidavit certifies that all adults living in the home and persons having legal custody of the children have not been convicted of criminal offenses listed in sub-section (E) of section 111 of the school code (see www.PHAA.com for details).

2. Parent designated as the "homeschool supervisor" must submit with the affidavit a high school diploma or G.E.D. certificate.

3. Parent must submit health and immunization records for each child.

4. Parent must submit a list of subjects to be taught and their objectives for each child. (The objective list can be derived from the Table of Contents of the textbooks used or the Scope and Sequence for each subject provided by most curriculum companies.)

B. By June 30 of each completed homeschooling year:

1. Parent must obtain a written evaluation from an educational professional (evaluator) who will review the child's completed work. The evaluation must be submitted to the school district's homeschool official with a portfolio of the child's completed work and a daily record of attendance (180

days or 900 hours for elementary students/990 hours for secondary level).

2. Parent must have each child who has completed 3rd, 5th, or 8th grade take a standardized achievement test. The results must be submitted to the school district with the evaluation.

Chapter 2:

Setting Up Your Homeschooling Program

One of the most common mistakes I've seen with families who fail at homeschooling is that the parent did not have the knowledge to start a homeschool program effectively and often prescribed a completely inappropriate curriculum for his child. Every child is different, many having academic needs that must be addressed with specialized and individual courses of instruction that are readily available for homeschoolers today.

Because money is always a big issue, some parents try to cut too many corners with their children's education. I've worked with families who did not commit themselves financially to provide an excellent program; thus, because of the lack of the proper tools, the children's academic achievement suffered greatly.

Discipline, or lack of it, has also reared its ugly head in failing homeschool scenarios. Before the first day of homeschooling ever arrives, parents need to establish the fact that school is "school," and both parents and children need to approach every day's assignments with that in mind. A wise parent will designate a room, or a table at least, as the homeschooling center where all homeschooling activities take place. Allowing a child to lie on the sofa in his pajamas and read "a book" until 11 a.m. is not formal school. Success demands organization, the setting up of goals, and the completion of them following a pre-designated time schedule at a pre-designated place. Only then will every family member feel that academic progress is being achieved.

This manual addresses all of the fore-mentioned problems facing homeschoolers, and then some. A parent who uses this manual faithfully and completes the following tasks increases his chances of having not only a successful year but also a happy one. Perhaps for the first time in his educational life, the child will learn from properly diagnosed materials and with adequate facilities and supplies. Frustration and negative attitudes will disappear and in their place, you'll have a child who actually wants to learn!

A. Tasks To Complete in June before You Start To Homeschool

(Date completed)

1. _____ Obtain all required affidavits and start-up paperwork from the local school district. Requirements differ in all states and vary from school district to school district within each state. (Sample affidavit in appendix, page 126.)

2. _____ Have each child take an achievement test to determine the grade level of achievement or "performance level" and areas of deficiency. Contact a homeschool consultant or your school district to find where the test can be taken. Many publishing companies also provide achievement test materials for parents who desire to administer the tests themselves. (See list of the most popular curriculum companies in Chapter 3.)

Name of test administrator_____

Phone number _____

E-mail _____

Date, Time, and Place Test Will Be Administered

_____

_____

_____

_____

Administration Fee_____

Achievement Test Results

Name of Test:_____

_____

Date Administered _____

Administered by _____

_____

Name of Child	Reading G.E.	Language G.E.	Math G.E.*
_____	_____	_____	_____
_____	_____	_____	_____
_____	_____	_____	_____
_____	_____	_____	_____
_____	_____	_____	_____
_____	_____	_____	_____

(* G.E. = the grade equivalency or the grade level at which your child is performing; will be calculated by the test administrator or the publishing company providing the tests.)

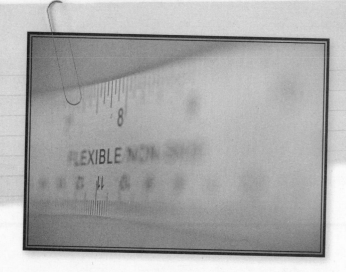

3. _____ Decide what method of homeschooling is best for your child(ren):

    A. Conventional Classroom: The child uses a prescribed curriculum, completes assignments, and takes tests on a regular basis to measure his mastery of the subject. (See Chapter 3 for the leading homeschool textbook publishers.)

        1. Texts — The year's content for each subject is included in one or two large student textbooks. May have accompanying workbooks, worksheets, tests, teacher's manual, and lesson plans.

        2. Packets — The year's content for each subject is divided into smaller "workbook-type"

manuals, 6 to 12 per subject per year. Tests are included.

B. Unit Studies: All subject matter for the year is presented in units of study that incorporate all disciplines around a central theme. Instead of texts providing all the information, the child learns through "hands-on" projects and library books, the level of difficulty is contingent on the child's *grade level of achievement* from his achievement test.

Example: A unit study about Indians in America would include:

Math: Conventional math exercises from a text or workbook plus learning methods Indians used to do calculations and figuring.

English: Reading and writing exercises include doing research about famous Indians, tribes, battles, etc., and writing compositions and/or giving short speeches about different tribes.

Social Studies: Exercises would include visiting the library or Internet and reading about the history of different American tribes. A sample project would be to construct a time-line when the tribes of America possessed the land.

Science & Health: Would include studying the Indians' close relationship with nature, their lifestyles and dependence on it. A sample project would be to make a poster displaying how Indians used all parts of a buffalo killed in a hunt.

Art: Includes projects such as building a model teepee, making bead jewelry, sketching and coloring different tribal designs and symbols.

Music: Includes learning different war chants, tom tom beats, and songs about Indians.

(Note: Certain publishing companies provide complete "Unit Studies" manuals and guides for parents. See Chapter 3.)

C. "Unschooling" Method ("Deschooling"): No textbooks or formal lesson plans are used. The children have access to resource materials from either a home library or public library and the Internet. The children are allowed to learn what they choose with the parent fulfilling the role of a monitor, not a teacher. Hands-on projects such as baking, building a birdhouse, or writing a composition about a trip to a museum take precedence over completing structured lessons and tests. Interaction with other homeschooling families to work on projects together is a vital part of this method. (For more information, go to www.sandradodd.com.)

B. Tasks To Complete in July before You Start to Homeschool

(Unnecessary if using the "Unschooling" method)

1._____ Designate a room in your house as your "classroom."

_____ Teacher's desk

_____ Daily record of attendance (logbook)

_____ Teacher's lesson plan book

_____ Manuals and test keys

_____ Student desk for each child or large table for all the children

_____ File cabinet and file folders for each child

_____ Equipment and supplies:

_____ Map or globe of world

_____ Pencils, paper, rulers, etc., for each child

_____ Dictionary, encyclopedia, computer

All supplies are available at office supply stores, discount stores, or online school supply companies such as:

Incentive Publications at
www.incentivepublications.com or 800.421.2830
The Teacher Store at
www.teacherstorehouse.com or 877.461.2002

(There are about 600 other "school supply" sites available online.)

2. _____ With your achievement test results, use the "Scope and Sequence" chart (Chapter 3) to order the appropriate curriculum (most popular curriculum companies are listed in Chapter 3) and grade level for each subject. *Important! A third grader does not necessarily perform on the third grade level in every subject:*

Name of Text & Company, Phone Number, Website (if text is needed)

Math _____
_____

English _____
_____

Soc. Stud. _____
_____

Science _____
_____

Health _____
_____

Art _____
_____

Music _____
_____

Phys. Ed. _____
_____

Other _____

(*Note: Some states such as Pennsylvania allow parents to borrow public school texts to use as homeschool curriculum. However, no lesson plans, answer keys, or tests are provided, thus making the use of public school texts extremely difficult, especially with high school subjects like algebra and chemistry.)

3. _____ Open files in a file cabinet with manila folders for each child.

   _____ One file per subject for tests to be taken. Place tests in files as soon as curriculum arrives. (*Curriculum in packet form usually has the test for each packet stapled in the center of the packet. Remove the test before the child works in the packet.)

   _____ One file per subject for completed tests.

   _____ One file per subject for completed assignments.

4. _____ Check with local school district concerning the deadline (if any) to submit homeschool registration documents and end-of-the-year reports to the state.

C. Tasks To Complete before or in August before You Start To Homeschool

1. _____ Submit homeschool registration documents to the state (usually done through the local public school district or a state-wide homeschooling association).

2. _____ Call a homeschool support group and notify them of your intent to become a member and participate in the meetings and activities planned for the year (vitally important).

3. _____ For parents of high school students desiring to earn a diploma, from your homeschool support group, find the names of any homeschooling accreditation agencies that grant credit and issue high school diplomas. Contact them and review their graduation requirements.

4. _____ For parents of high school students desiring to earn a diploma, check with homeschool curriculum publishing companies to find those that offer an accreditation program and issue high school diplomas. Contact them and review their graduation requirements.

5. _____ Decide if your child should earn a diploma or take a G.E.D. when he completes high school requirements. Contact your local school district for G.E.D. information.

Keep list of agencies' or companies' requirements in the back of this book.

Duplicate following form as needed.

****

_____(name of child) will earn a high school diploma in the year _____.

Name of accreditation agency or publishing company. ____

_____

_____

Address_____

Phone Number_____

Contact Person_____

E-mail _____

_____ (name of child) will earn his G.E.D. in the year _____.

School or place where test will be taken._____

_____

Address_____

Time of year test is given _____

_____

Contact Person_____

_____

Phone Number _____

_____

E-mail _____

****

D. Tasks To Complete from August until June as You Homeschool

1. _____ Homeschool following your daily lesson plans that are purchased from the curriculum company of your choice. Record in a daily log all days of attendance, absences, field trips, and a brief description and dates of all assignments and special projects completed.

2. _____ Review quarterly the state requirements for attendance and curriculum and evaluate if you are fulfilling the requirements.

_____ 1st quarter: Requirements fulfilled
Requirements not fulfilled (list):_____

_____

_____

_____

_____ 2nd quarter: Requirements fulfilled
Requirements not fulfilled (list):_____

_____

_____

_____

_____ 3rd quarter: Requirements fulfilled
Requirements not fulfilled (list):_____

_____

_____

_____

_____ 4th quarter: Requirements fulfilled
Requirements not fulfilled (list):_____

_____

_____

_____

3. _____ If state requires portfolio of child's progress, purchase three-ring binder with colored tab dividers, one for each of child's subjects.

4. _____ Every quarter, place samples of completed assignments, tests, and project work in appropriate subject division in portfolio.

_____ 1st quarter: Requirements fulfilled
Requirements not fulfilled (list):_____

_____

_____

_____

_____ 2nd quarter: Requirements fulfilled

Requirements not fulfilled (list): _____

_____

_____

_____

_____ 3rd quarter: Requirements fulfilled

Requirements not fulfilled (list): _____

_____

_____

_____

_____ 4th quarter: Requirements fulfilled

Requirements not fulfilled (list): _____

_____

_____

_____

Chapter 3

Chapter 3:

Curriculum and Legal Help

A. Scope and Sequence

Although homeschool curriculum publishing companies differ slightly with their list of subjects and objectives per grade level, they all follow a national standard accepted by most schools and academic institutions. Following is a generic Scope and Sequence, which can be used as a guide to determine what subjects your child should be learning in every grade. (Most publishing companies provide their own complete Scope and Sequence upon request.) The core curriculum subjects are the major subjects that are taught every day. Auxiliary subjects are those that are usually taught once or twice a week at the parents' discretion.

A List of Subjects Taught at Each Grade Level from Kindergarten through Twelfth Grade

Five-Year-Old Kindergarten Scope and Sequence

*Note: The actual content presented in each subject per year varies with every curriculum publishing company. Contact the publishing company of your choice for a copy of its Scope and Sequence.

Core Curriculum Taught Every School Day

Following is a sample of the content presented in each subject.

Phonics (includes alphabet recognition, phonics sounds, simple word recognition)

Math (includes shapes, colors, measurement, money, counting)

Penmanship (includes printing letters, coloring, printing his/her name)

Social Studies and Science (includes identifying community helpers, simple lessons about animals, plants, space, weather)

Auxiliary Subjects

Art (projects using different media contingent on child's ability)

Music (voice or instrumental training and beginning music theory contingent on child's ability)

Physical Education (organized playtime or exercise periods contingent on child's ability)

Health (personal hygiene, food pyramid and nutrition, manners, safety issues)

First Grade Scope and Sequence

Core Curriculum

(Important: Textbooks for every year **MUST** be prescribed on child's *performance level* contingent on achievement test results, not necessarily child's actual grade.):

Phonics and Spelling

Reading

Math

Penmanship

Social Studies: History and Geography

Science and Health, Safety

Auxiliary Subjects

Art

Music

Physical Education

Second Grade Scope and Sequence

Core Curriculum

Language Arts: Phonics, Spelling, Grammar

Reading

Math

Penmanship

Social Studies: History and Geography

Science, Health and Safety

Auxiliary Subjects

Art

Music

Physical Education

Third Grade Scope and Sequence

Core Curriculum

Language Arts: Phonics, Spelling, Grammar, Poetry

Reading

Math

Penmanship

Social Studies: History and Geography

Science

Health and Safety

Auxiliary Subjects

Art

Music

Physical Education

Fourth Grade Scope and Sequence

Core Curriculum

Language Arts: Phonics, Spelling, Grammar, Poetry,
    Creative Writing

Reading and Literature

Math

Penmanship

Social Studies: History and Geography

Science

Health and Safety

Auxiliary Subjects

Art

Music

Physical Education

Fifth Grade Scope and Sequence

Core Curriculum

Language Arts: Spelling, Grammar, Poetry, Creative Writing
Reading and Literature
Math
Penmanship
Social Studies: History and Geography
Science
Health and Safety

Auxiliary Subjects

Art
Music
Physical Education

Sixth Grade Scope and Sequence

Core Curriculum

Language Arts: Spelling, Grammar, Poetry, Writing Skills
Reading and Literature
Math
Penmanship
Social Studies: History and Geography
Science
Health and Safety

Auxiliary Subjects
Art
Music
Physical Education

Seventh Grade Scope and Sequence

Core Curriculum

Language Arts: Grammar and Composition
Literature and Poetry
Math
History (including one semester of state history)
Geography
Science
Health (including pertinent teen issues)

Auxiliary Subjects

Art
Music
Physical Education

Eighth Grade Scope and Sequence

Core Curriculum

Language Arts: Grammar and Composition
Literature and Poetry
Math (Pre-algebra for advanced students)

History (including one semester of state history if not
    covered in 7th)
Science
Health (including pertinent teen issues)

Auxiliary Subjects

Art

Music
Physical Education

HIGH SCHOOL SUBJECTS FOR EARNED CREDIT

Ninth Grade (Freshman) Scope and Sequence

(* Important: Textbooks for every year **MUST** be prescribed
on child's *performance level* contingent on achievement test
results, not necessarily child's actual grade. If a child per-
forms below grade level, he still earns credit and is classified
as a "general course" student.)

Core Curriculum

(Taught every day for at least 45 minutes: 1 credit each.)
Note: Accreditation standards vary in different states. Check
your state requirements.

Language Arts 9: Grammar, Composition, Literature,
    Poetry

Math

    General Course: General Math

    Business Course: General Math Fundamentals

    Academic Course: Algebra 1

(*Note: The academic course is the college preparatory course.)

World Geography/World History

Science:

    General Course: General Science

    Business Course: General Science or Biology

    Academic Course: Biology

Electives: (e.g., New Testament Survey, Oceanography, Psychology)

Auxiliary Subjects

(Taught one to two hours a week at parent's discretion or state requirements.) Note: Accreditation standards vary in different states.

One Hour: ¼ Credit; Two Hours Per Week: ½ Credit

Health (including pertinent teen issues)

Art

Music

Physical Education

Life Skills, Homemaking

One Semester Electives

Tenth Grade (Sophomore) Scope and Sequence

(* Important: Textbooks for every year **MUST** be prescribed on child's *performance level* contingent on achievement test results, not necessarily child's actual grade.)

Core Curriculum

(Taught every day for at least 45 minutes: 1 credit each.)
Note: Accreditation standards vary in different states.

Language Arts 10: Grammar, Composition, Literature, Poetry

Math:

General Course: Basic Math

Business Course: Consumer Math

Academic Course: Algebra 2

American History

Science:

General Course: Basic Science

Business Course: General Science

Academic Course: Physical Science

Electives

Auxiliary Subjects

(Taught one to two hours a week at parent's discretion or state requirements.) Note: Accreditation standards vary in different states.

One Hour: ¼ Credit; Two Hours Per Week: ½ Credit

Art

Music

Physical Education

Life Skills, Homemaking

One Semester Electives

Eleventh Grade (Junior) Scope and Sequence

(* Important: Textbooks for every year **MUST** be prescribed on child's *performance level* contingent on achievement test results, not necessarily child's actual grade.)

Core Curriculum

(Taught every day for at least 45 minutes: 1 credit each.)

Note: Accreditation standards vary in different states.

Language Arts 11: Grammar, Composition, Literature,
   Poetry

Math:

   General Course: Consumer Math

   Business Course: Business Math

   Academic Course: Plane Geometry

Civics and Government

Science:

   General Course: Biology or Science Elective of
      Student's Choice

   Business Course: Science Elective of Student's Choice

   Academic Course: Chemistry (Alg. 1 a Prerequisite)

Foreign Language: Academic Course Students

Electives

Auxiliary Subjects

(Taught one to two hours a week at parent's discretion or state requirements.) Note: Accreditation standards vary in different states.

One Hour: ¼ Credit; Two Hours Per Week: ½ Credit

Art

Music

Physical Education

Life Skills, Homemaking

One Semester Electives

Twelfth Grade (Senior) Scope and Sequence

(* Important: Textbooks for every year **MUST** be prescribed on child's *performance level* contingent on achievement test results, not necessarily child's actual grade.)

Core Curriculum

(Taught every day for at least 45 minutes: 1 credit each.)
Note: Accreditation standards vary in different states.

Language Arts 12: Grammar, Composition, Literature, Poetry

Math:

    General Course: Requirements Fulfilled

    Business Course: Requirements Fulfilled; Alg. 1 recommended

    Academic Course: Plane Trigonometry and Analytical Geometry

History:

    General Course: Requirements Fulfilled

    Business Course: Requirements Fulfilled

    Academic Course: Economics

Science:

    General Course: Requirements Fulfilled

    Business Course: Requirements Fulfilled

    Academic Course: Physics

Foreign Language: Academic Course Students

Electives

Auxiliary Subjects

(Taught one to two hours a week at parent's discretion or state requirements.) Note: Accreditation standards vary in different states.

One Hour: ¼ Credit; Two Hours Per Week: ½ Credit

Art

Music

Physical Education

Life Skills, Homemaking

One Semester Electives

B. The Most Popular Homeschool Curricula in the United States

The key to a child's homeschooling success lies with the parents' decision to purchase the appropriate curriculum that meets the needs of each child in the family. Once you've decided what type of homeschooling method you want to use (see Chapter 2), you can purchase textbooks and supplementary materials, including videos, CDs, satellite and computer programs, and audiovisual aids for any subject on any grade level from numerous publishing companies in the United States. Many of these companies also provide achievement test materials for parents who desire to administer the tests themselves.

Following is a list of the most popular and widely used companies (mostly Christian) that provide textbooks and educational materials for homeschoolers. I've included the companies' websites (if available) and their phone numbers. I've also rated the level of difficulty concerning how the subject matter is presented in the different curricula and the demands each one makes on the students (my opinion derived from years of experience reviewing educational materials). A rating of N/O reflects "no opinion" based on my lack of knowledge concerning that particular company's products. The rating in no way reflects the quality of the material presented.

Difficulty Rating based on Author's Professional Opinion

Scale: 1 (Easier to Complete) to 10 (Most Challenging) (in alphabetical order)

Company Information — Level of Difficulty

A BEKA Books — 10
www.abeka.com
Pensacola, FL; Phone: 877-223-5226

Accelerated Christian Education (packets) — 7
www.schooloftomorrow.com
Lewisville, TX; Phone: 800-925-7777

Alpha Omega — 7
www.AOP.com
Chandler, AZ; Phone: 800-622-3070

(Includes "Switched on Schoolhouse," "Lifepacs," "Weaver Curriculum")
*Has state history for all 50 states

Apologia Educational Ministries (Science) — 9
www.apologia.com
Anderson, IN; Phone: 888-524-4724

Bob Jones University Press — 10
www.bjup.com
Greenville, SC; Phone: 800-845-5731

Bright Minds, The Critical Thinking Company — 7
www.BrightMinds.us
Coos Bay, OR; Phone: 800-641-6555

Christian Light Publications (Mennonite) — 6
www.clp.org
Harrisonburg, VA; Phone: 800-776-0478

Easy Grammar — N/O
www.easygrammar.com
Scottsdale, AZ; Phone: 800-641-6015

KONOS (Unit Studies) — 7
www.konos.com
Anna, TX

Math-U-See — 6
www.MathUSee.com
USA and Canada, Phone: 888-854-6284

Rod and Staff Publishers, Inc. (Mennonite) — 5
www.rodstaff.com
Crockett, KY; Phone: 606-522-4896

Rosetta Stone, Inc. (Foreign Languages) — N/O
www.rosettastone.com
Harrisonburg, VA; Phone: 800-788-0822

Saxon Math (Secular Company) — 8
www.saxonpublishers.harcourtachieve.com/en-US/saxonpublishers.htm
Austin, TX; Phone: 800-531-5015

Sonlight Curriculum — 6
www.sonlight.com
Littleton, CO; Phone: 303-730-6292

Shurley English — 6
www.shurley.com
Cabot, AR; Phone: 800-566-2966

C. Additional Curriculum Websites and Phone Numbers

Buy, Sell, Trade, or Rent Homeschool Curriculum

The Homeschooler's Curriculum Swap (also includes forums); online service: www.theswap.com

Laurelwood Publications
www.laurelwoodbooks.com
Bluemont, VA; Phone: 540-554-2670

New Curriculum and Supplies for Every Subject on Any Grade Level

Alfred Publishing Co, Inc. (Music)
www.alfred.com
Van Nuys, CA; Phone: 800-292-6122

Christian Liberty Academy School System
www.homeschools.org
Arlington Heights, IL; Phone: 301-263-2700

Handwriting Without Tears
www.hwtears.com
Cabin John, MD; Phone: 888-983-8409

The Homeschooling Book Club
www.HomeschoolingBooks.com
Fenton, MI; Phone: 800-421-6645

Home School Resource Exchange
www.hsresourceexchange.com
Lemoyne, PA; Phone: 717-612-1516

The Homeschool Super Center
www.homeschoolsupercenter.com

How Great Thou Art Publications (Art Projects)
www.howgreathouart.com
McFarlan, NC; Phone: 800-982-3729

The Learnables on Computer (Foreign Languages)
www.learnables.com
Kansas City, MO; Phone: 800-237-1830

Master Books (evolution-free)
Unit study/supplementary materials, free downloads and educational guides
www.masterbooks.net
Green Forest, AR 800-999-3777

Quality Science Labs, LLC (Chemistry Labs)
Biology, Physics, Physical Science, Organic Chemistry
www.qualitysciencelabs.com
Lake George, CO; Phone: 866-700-1884

Switched on Schoolhouse (State History)
Alpha Omega Press
www.AOP.com
Rock Rapids, IA; Phone: 800-622-3070

Veritas Press ("Classics" Books Specialty)
www.VeritasPress.com
Lancaster, PA; Phone: 800-922-5082

Vision Video (Videos and DVDs)
www.visionvideo.com
Worchester, PA; Phone: 800-523-0226

The Vision Forum (History)
www.visionforum.com
San Antonio, TX Phone: 800-440-0022

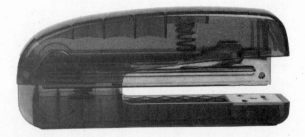

D. Advanced Placement (AP) Courses
(for advanced high school students)

High school students who have no trouble completing their high school subjects might want to consider taking AP Courses. AP Courses are college-level courses taken as a part of a high school program. These courses offer advanced students who have completed all their state requirements for a high school diploma the opportunity to take courses with more challenging college-level content. Students who complete AP courses are eligible to take the AP exams, administered each May by the College Board. These exams are scored on a scale of 1–5. Students scoring between a 3 and 5 may qualify for college credit at most colleges and universities.

Why Take AP Courses?

There are many reasons to take AP courses:
- Demonstrate to college admissions officers your ability to excel in college-level coursework
- Emphasize your commitment to academic pursuits
- Prepare for the AP exams and the possibility of receiving college credit at schools nationwide

Who May Take AP Courses?

If you are a junior or senior in high school, you have successfully completed advanced courses in core subjects (including successful completion of an honors course), and you are college-bound, then consider enrollment options for AP courses.

For more information go to:
www.collegeboard.com
or www.keystonehighschool.com
Phone: 877-877-8470

E. Legal Counsel

Christian families who consider educating their children in the nurture and admonition of the Lord as a mandate from God himself should not have the concern of interference from any outside organization, particularly the government. Although mostly all homeschooling families want to be free from the restrictive requirements that any state law might impose, a few families have strong religious convictions against any government control whatsoever.

If, perchance, local and/or state officials question the legality of any facet of your homeschooling program, professional Christian legal counsel is readily available by contacting:

The Home School Legal Defense Association
One Patrick Henry Circle
Purcellville, VA 20132
540-338-5600
Fax: 540-338-2733
Website: www.hslda.org

Chapter 4:

Helpful Resources for Parents

Wise is the parent who investigates to the fullest extent what his options are to homeschool his children successfully. The educational market has an ample supply of homeschooling guides and manuals to help parents make informative decisions as they begin their academic venture. Following is a sample of the books available that offer help on all facets of homeschooling. (The list reflects 2007 prices.)

A. How-To Books for Parents

Beyond Survival: A Guide to Abundant Life Homeschooling

by Diana Waring listed at www.dianawaring.com (217 pages at $12.99)

Beyond Survival gives you the author's personal experience on the written page. She offers the preparation and working plan for a successful homeschooling experience. With confidence and compassionate humor, she leads the reader on a joy-filled educational journey.

Christian Homeschooling (Foundation and Practice)

— listed in "Christian Liberty Press Catalog 2005–06" (128 pages at $4.95) www.christianlibertybooks.co.za

This book provides parents with a wealth of information on how to operate a homeschool. Issues discussed include philosophy and methodology.

Dr. Beechick's Homeschool Answer Book

by Dr. Ruth Beechick listed at www.amazon.com (218 pages at $11.00)

This book addresses topics such as:

1. Are unit studies the best approach to multilevel teaching?
2. How should I teach the times tables?
3. What should I do when I'm helping my older children and my kindergartner keeps saying he's bored?

It answers frequently asked questions regarding curriculum, learning theory, the Three R's, special education, family life, and more.

Easy Homeschooling Companion: Exhortation, Encouragement, and Ideas

by Lorraine Curry; paperback; listed at www.graceandtruthbooks.com (265 pages at $18.95)

This book is packed with tips and ideas to help any homeschool grow in character, grace, and high standards. A devotional and homeschool "how-to" book rolled into one.

The First Year of Homeschooling Your Child: Your Complete Guide to Getting off to the Right Start

by Linda Dobson listed on www.christianbook.com (360 pages at $12.99)

The book covers learning styles, homeschooling myths, deschooling, learning readiness, and more. A unique feature is the chapter that presents "a week in the life" profiles of families using various homeschooling methods. Scattered throughout are highlighted tips on the topic, "What I wish someone had

told me during my first year of homeschooling." The book includes learning resources, the "weirdest homeschooling laws" segment, and state-by-state legal information.

Homeschooling for Success

by Robert T. Kiyosaki, and Rebecca Kochenderfer listed on www.amazon.com (320 pages at $18.99)

This resource is filled with many homeschooling resources as well as insight on learning styles and different kinds of intelligences to help a parent figure out which kind of homeschooling style would best suit his or her child. It gives advice on homeschooling at different age levels, as well as college and un-college alternatives as well.

Mary Pride's Complete Guide to Getting Started in Homeschooling

by Mary Pride listed at www.christianbook.com (600 pages at $23.40)

This 600-page volume provides families with everything they could possibly need to know to start schooling. It discusses topics such as:

1. The advantages of homeschooling
2. Common misconceptions
3. Practical information on methods and materials
4. Planning and record keeping
5. Testing
6. Special needs and gifted children

The McGraw-Hill Homeschooling Companion

by Julie Gattis and Laura Saba listed at www.amazon.com (288 pages from $4.01)

A guide for the parents of children from the primary years through high school, it covers different approaches to homeschooling as well as the specific methods for setting up the home learning environment, including legal requirements, supplies, and lesson plans. Core curriculum planning, computer use, and achievement testing are covered. It also includes ten favorite homeschool suppliers, websites, and homeschool laws for all 50 states.

The Successful Homeschool Family Handbook

by Dr. Raymond and Dorothy Moore; listed at www.half-pricehomeschool.com (170 pages at $5.00)

This book's topics include choosing a curriculum that really works for the child, avoiding student resentment and parent burnout, targeting the child's interest and motivation to make learning fun, helping the child excel in educational goals (including standardized tests), understanding how a child's developmental stages contribute to learning and seeing the big picture of family and society in the learning process.

Things We Wish We had Known

compiled and edited by Bill and Diana Waring listed at www.christianbook.com (227 pages at $9.99)

This book makes available to novices, long-timers, and parents just starting the time-earned secrets of 50 veteran homeschooling families. Pioneers and leaders in the homeschooling community discuss the concepts, the basics, the priorities, God's involvement, Christian characters, and the blessings.

What Your Child Needs to Know When
by Robin Sampson; listed at www.christianbook.com (312 pages at $19.99)

Covered in this book are topics such as:
1. What are the state requirements?
2. What are God's requirements?
3. How children were taught in Bible times.
4. How to prepare goals for the year.
5. Making the Bible the core of all teaching.
6. How Greek philosophy influenced public education.

B. Help for Special Needs Children

Many parents with special needs children have opted to homeschool because of the frustration the entire family has faced with other educational alternatives that have not met the needs of the child. Those parents' greatest concern is whether their children are getting the proper and adequate training they need in a specialized homeschool environment.

Fortunately, there are numerous organizations available today to help special needs families. Following is a partial list of those services available:

Christian Cottage Schools
3560 W. Dawson Rd., Sedalia, CO 80135
Phone: 303-688-6626 / 1-888-286-5494
www.christiancottage.com
Mike and Terry Spray offer a national education service that includes testing, curriculum design, lesson planning, unit lessons, workshops, and ongoing counseling.

Exceptional Diagnostics
220 Douglas Drive, Simpsonville, SC 29681
Phone: 864-967-4729
www.edtesting.com
Joe Sutton, PhD, is a certified educational diagnostician who provides individual educational testing services including psycho-educational evaluations and career testing. He also writes IEPs (Individual Educational Programs) and conducts teleconferences.

Family and Education Consulting Service
10340 B Kidron Ave., Englewood, FL 34224
Phone: 941-460-0707
Bob Beninger offers testing, curriculum consulting, and counseling for families homeschooling a special needs child.

The Home School Foundation
Purcellville, VA
Phone: 540-338-8688
www.homeschoolfoundation.org

This group provides assistance to needy families such as widows who homeschool, special needs children, and seniors needing financial help for college.

Joni and Friends
P.O. Box 3333, Agoura Hills, CA 90301
www.joniandfriends.org

This organization offers a free monthly newsletter. They sponsor family camps in the summer, where attendant care is provided for the physically challenged.

Learning Products and Services
Phone: 800-745-8212
joyceoffice@aol.com
www.joyceherzog.com (click "Services")

Joyce Herzog provides telephone or in-home consultations. She draws upon thirty-five years experience to offer creative and proven suggestions and resources for struggling learners.

National Challenged Homeschoolers Associated Network
P.O. Box 39, Porthill, ID 83853
Phone: 208-267-6246
www.nathhan.com

This is a national organization of homeschooling parents with special needs children. NATHHAN coordinators Tom and Sherry Bushnell publish NATHHAN News, an easy-to-use Internet magazine.

National Dissemination Center for Children with Disabilities (NICHCY)

P.O. Box 1492, Washington, DC 20013
Phone: 800-695-0285
www.nichcy.org
This organization offers free information for families who have a child with a special need.

National Institute for Learning Disabilities (NILD)
107 Seekel St., Norfolk VA 23505
Contact Janet Fish at 757-423-8646 / 877-661-6453
www.nild.net
NILD provides workshops and educational therapy in Christian school settings for learning disabled children. There are also some NILD therapists in private practice.

Parents Instructing Challenged Children (PICC)
c/o Mulvey, 700 W. Liberty St., Rome, NY 13440-3942
Phone: 315-339-5524
www.piccnys.com
This organization serves parents of special needs children in New York state.

The International Dyslexia Association
Chester Building, Suite 382
8600 LaSalle Rd., Baltimore, MD 21286-2044
www.interdys.org

This association is a source of helpful information for those who have difficulty reading.

Wayside Language Center
12721 NE 101st Place, Kirkland, WA 98033
Phone: 425-822-2772

Consultation services are offered by Dr. John Blanchard. He also helps parents plan educational goals for special needs children.

C. Other Great Websites for Homeschoolers

www.bridgewayacademy.com
Phone: 800-863-1474

Resources, discounts, tips, evaluation tests, and a diploma program for homeschoolers.

www.centerpointacademy.com

A full-service Military High School Correspondence Academy that focuses on those striving to meet enlistment requirements in the U.S. Armed Services.

www.christianedusa.com

Dictionary, encyclopedia, thesaurus, Bible, Bible dictionary information and newspapers, Internet filters, and resource
links to help aid in the homeschooling process.

www.clickatutor.us/Go

Find out about the world's foremost Cyber school (Cyber school — a homeschooling program conducted on the
Internet).

www.curriculumexpress.com

Purchase discount curriculum online with next day shipping.

www.GEDPrepOnline.com

Preparation, practice, and news about recent changes for
those wanting to take the G.E.D. test.

www.homeschoolmall.net

An array of online "storefronts" selling products and services for all student needs.

www.icerb.org

International Cyber Educational Review Board. Learn
about the Cyber Academy.

www.ldhope.com

The Essential Learning Institute offers help to any child with any learning problem.

www.rsts.net

The Homeschooling Resource Center of Homeschool Families offers links and resource sites to all kinds of information about class subjects and education in general (the encyclopedia of educational links).

Chapter 5:

Starting Your Own Homeschool Support Group

One of the main criticisms of homeschooling by those looking from the outside in is that every homeschooling family is an island unto itself with the children suffering from isolation from the world around them and a severe lack of social interaction.

Although the perspective from the homeschooling family is usually quite the opposite, homeschooling parents often find themselves in a constant war against the clock. As they try to teach a full homeschooling curriculum to their child(ren) daily, they often at the same time must care for their preschool children, cook meals, go to doctors, and just try to maintain a level of sanity and organization within the home environment itself.

All homeschooling parents understand the need to develop socialization skills in their children, but to take the steps necessary to initiate and administer worthwhile activities with others outside of the immediate family can be too time consuming and expensive for the average homeschooling parent to consider.

Christian families have an advantage in that they have a strong support system in their local church with activities and fellowship offered several times a week. There are community clubs such as the Boy Scouts and sports teams that also afford the homeschooling family an opportunity to interact with others. But one of the best options, a homeschooling support group, is usually the most affordable and effective way to involve the entire family in exciting social events outside the home. Like-minded parents who involve themselves in a homeschooling support group find the camaraderie and encouragement they themselves need as well as plenty of interaction for their children in a variety of different activities throughout the school year.

If there is no homeschool support group in a family's immediate area, a parent always has the option to start his/her own group. Although it is a challenge for a first-year homeschooling family to also tackle such a task, starting a local group is not impossible.

If you have the desire to start a local group and feel that God wants you to be the "foreman," this manual has a checklist of suggestions that will help the initiation and functioning of the group to run more smoothly. As you contemplate starting your group, consider the following steps, ask God to give you clear direction, and take that first step!

Tasks to Complete as You Start Your Homeschool Support Group

(Record the date after completion)

(Date completed)

1. _____ Just start! Find other homeschooling parents in your area and plan to spend some informal time together, perhaps once a week: meet at the playground, go on a short field trip together, meet at each other's house for an art project or game time, etc.

OTHER HOMESCHOOLING FAMILIES IN MY AREA

Name, Address, Phone Number, E-mail

_____

_____

_____

_____

_____

_____

_____

2. _____ Consider getting more organized. Ask several families to commit to becoming involved.

HOMESCHOOLING FAMILIES WHO WILL BECOME INVOLVED

Name, Address, Phone Number, E-mail

_____

_____

_____

_____

_____

_____

_____

3. _____ Ask God into your meetings. Pray as a group when you meet and have a devotional time.

4. _____ Choose a convenient meeting time for the group (i.e., once a week on Friday afternoons, twice a month on Monday afternoons, etc.) and name the group.

OUR HOMESCHOOLING SUPPORT GROUP'S NAME

_____

_____

will meet

_____

5. _____ Write a basic "statement of faith" containing commonly held religious beliefs with supporting scriptures.

****

A Sample "Statement of Faith"

The Bible is the inspired and infallible Word of God and is God's complete and final revelation to man. In its original autographs, the Bible is without error in whole and in part.

God has existed from all eternity in three persons: God the Father, God the Son, and God the Holy Spirit. Jesus Christ came to earth as God in human flesh and was fully God and fully man, except without sin.

All men have violated God's righteous requirements and His holy character; therefore, all mankind is under God's wrath, judgment, and just condemnation.

Jesus Christ came to earth for one central purpose, to pay the penalty for man's sin through His substitutionary atoning death on the Cross. His subsequent visible resurrection attests to His successful accomplishment of that work which was ordained by God before the foundations of the world.

The only way to heaven is through salvation by the grace of God, a gift freely given to the sinner. The sinner must respond by individual faith in the sacrificial death and shed blood of Christ alone and must not trust in any personal works whatsoever to gain eternal life.

6. _____ Decide on a mission statement and why you want to meet. Is it strictly for fellowship? For support? For educational opportunities?

****

A Sample Mission Statement

_____ (Name of group) is a distinctly Christian organization with a statement of faith that exists to render support and encouragement to Christian parents who homeschool their children of all ages. The group also seeks to provide for the children educational and fun activities that are wholesome and character developing as well as social, yet completely within the parameters of Judeo-Christian principles. This organization also holds to the biblical tenets that parents are totally responsible for their children's education and that spiritual training is of the utmost priority.

****

7. _____ Form a leadership hierarchy. One person can run a small group effectively, but for a large group a hierarchy works best. A small board or committee of dedicated individuals should meet regularly to make important decisions with a president having the final say.

8. _____ Make governing bylaws at the start, which prevents problems later. (Once members start attending, requirements are hard to change without offenses or even legal ramifications.)

A. Choose leaders — How are future leaders selected and what criteria should they meet? Do they need to feel "called by God" and/or voted in? Who will be allowed to teach classes to your children?

B. Open or closed group — "Closed" means that all members have to meet a certain criteria or must agree to certain requirements. "Open" means that any homeschooling family can come.

C. Financial decisions — Should each family pay membership dues? Will expenses be met through fundraising or will you be a non-profit organization?

D. Rules for behavior — What are the guidelines for both parents and children? What action will be taken when parents can't control themselves or their children? (Sometimes, for example, parents' anger at ball games is an embarrassment to everyone.)

9. _____ Find a place to meet. (Churches, libraries, community buildings, Christian schools with gym facilities, etc.)

OUR SUPPORT GROUP WILL MEET AT:

Name of Building_____

Address_____

_____

Contact Person_____

Phone Number_____

10. _____ Consider individual homeschoolers' needs. As you plan activities, become acquainted with special needs and struggles. Look for activities and programs that will help all homeschoolers in the group.

11. _____ Use good communication:

A. Start a monthly newsletter — senior high students can take charge.

B. A phone and/or e-mail chain provides last-minute communication about upcoming events or changes in the schedule.

C. Start a member directory with parents' names, children's names and ages, and curricula used. Include leaders' names with phone numbers and e-mails and activities planned for the year.

D. Give each new member a copy of the group's statement of faith, mission statement, and bylaws.

12. _____ Provide educational opportunities that stimulate the children's creativity and understanding of difficult subjects.

Examples:

A. Art — plan group art classes that focus on either fine arts or crafts (e.g., a talented mother can volunteer her time to teach clay sculpture or families can pool resources to hire an art teacher).

B. Music — a professional musician or degreed music teacher will sometimes travel to an area to give lessons. Group musical events, such as talent shows, Christmas cantatas, or choral performances enhance the homeschool experience.

C. "Emergency Team Day" — schedule demonstrations with emergency personnel such as:

   1. State troopers with a police car and/or a helicopter

   2. EMTs with emergency vehicles and ambulances

   3. The Red Cross or personnel who specialize in CPR training

D. Science Fairs — with little organizational skill required, they are great motivators for learning. In a large room, set up tables for the displays. Have each student explain his display to the group. Award certificates for participation. (Many science curricula explain the details for students to complete science projects.)

E. Field Trips — contingent on time restraints and financial feasibility, plan trips to post offices, fire companies, historical sites, museums, factories, and amusement parks.

F. Learning Co-ops — in a classroom setting, children experience a group situation and make new friends. Difficult high school subjects, physical education classes, music, science labs, etc., can be offered.

13. _____ Provide helpful services. Homeschool groups can do some things that individuals have trouble doing alone.

A. Act as a liaison between homeschool families and the public school. Public schools that are required to offer services by state law welcome a support group's coordination of those services. Examples:

   1. Notification for health screening

   2. Registration for sports teams

B. Act as a liaison between homeschoolers and private schools that offer homeschoolers the opportunity to participate in classes or activities.

C. Sponsor group achievement testing. Employ the services of a qualified individual to test the group and purchase test booklets, directions, and scoring from a testing service.

D. Schedule a school photo shoot. Contact a local photographer; send out order sheets to all homeschooling families ahead of time.

E. Plan a meeting for new homeschoolers and families considering homeschooling. Share information about the laws in your state and how to start. Incorporate a curriculum display with experienced people to answer questions.

F. Have a used curriculum sale and/or exchange books with other families who no longer need their texts.

The key to running a successful homeschool support group is dedication and organization. The workload should not fall on the shoulders of one family. All families need to volunteer to contribute in some way and then fulfill their assigned responsibilities.

A willing spirit to work produces an organization in which every member of every family can benefit. At the end of each year, a group evaluation should bring to the forefront those activities that were worthwhile and helpful as well as those that seemed to benefit only a few. Suggestions from all the members to improve the group will only add to its success in the future as more families join and more activities are added to the yearly plan. With God's help, your homeschooling support group will be something of which you can be proud.

(Some information in this section is compliments of Sandy Sieber from her article "A Strong Support," unpublished as of July 30, 2007.)

Chapter 6:

A Word about Cyber Schools

A method of educating children at home that is growing in popularity is the "cyber school" or "virtual charter school." This type of specialized school is offered either by public schools or cyber charter schools that have contracts with school districts or other charter school authorizers. A school such as this offers online courses for children from kindergarten to the senior high school level.

The cyber school provides students with a computer, printer, and other educational supplies needed for each student. The instruction for each grade and class is delivered through the Internet. The curriculum is chosen and provided by the public school and/or charter school. "Religious" curriculum of any kind is usually not an option.

Students must be disciplined to complete assignments on a time schedule similar to that of a conventional classroom at a regular school. Parents of younger children must be heavily involved to monitor the children's daily progress in the comprehension of the material and the completion of homework assignments. A cyber school faculty is available to answer questions either online or by phone and to grade all written work.

Cyber school students are **NOT** considered homeschoolers because they are considered full time students of a bona fide "school" and are accountable to that organization's rules, guidelines, and curriculum demands.

Chapter 7:

What Will Everyone Else Think?

The decision a family makes to start homeschooling has far-reaching repercussions. As you make the commitment, purchase curriculum, and start rearranging your house to be more homeschool friendly, you can prepare for a variety of reactions, not only from your family members and friends but also from your own emotions.

Regardless of the firm commitment you will make to take such a major step with the academic lives of your children, doubts may assail in the form of negative opinions, some that you might never have expected.

To help prepare you for the reality check that will undoubtedly invade your peace of mind after approximately three weeks of homeschooling, the following list presents eight "surprising" responses that can discourage a homeschooling parent to such a degree that he/she will consider throwing in the towel. However, with a firm resolve, any parent can withstand the negative pressures from all sides and continue homeschooling his/her children for the glory of God. Long before the first day of homeschooling, the committed parent needs to decide that if God has called the family to homeschool, the family will not quit, no matter how many negative opinions surface.

"Reality Check"
(Will These Negative Opinions Make You Quit?)

1. Your parents schedule psychological testing for you and your spouse.

2. Your neighbors threaten to report you to the public school truant officer.

3. Your children miss their friends and want to go to a "real" school.

4. Your children don't want to get out of bed before 10:00 a.m. and they constantly fight.

5. Your children keep saying they "don't get it" after you've explained every new concept twenty times.

6. You haven't been able to complete one full day's set of lesson plans because of sickness, "emergencies," phone calls, and unforeseen family needs.

7. You haven't cleaned the house in six weeks and can't find two teachers' manuals with all the tests for the entire year.

8. You've discovered that homeschooling takes a disciplined lifestyle, a tight schedule, and brash determination on your part but no one appreciates what you're doing.

Parent, be prepared, and don't be surprised when the tide of unpopular opinion floods your home. Just ask God to help you and keep on keeping on!

Chapter 8:

Tools To Help You Organize

In working with homeschoolers and evaluating a variety of both excellent and poor home study programs, I have discovered a single entity present in those programs that worked like well-oiled machines. In only a short time I decided to adopt a "signature slogan," one that I've repeated more times to homeschooling families than I can possibly count:

"The key to successful homeschooling is organization."

Homeschooling families who keep accurate and organized records, document attendance, file completed homework, and budget their time effectively *will* be successful in their educational program. However, those who throw everything in a cardboard box at the end of every school day and dig it out the next are heading for nothing but frustration and academic disaster.

Because accurate record keeping is such an essential part of an effective homeschooling program, I've included

a section in this manual for parents to keep accurate records and have them readily available. The manual is designed so that important documents can also be included.

Your Records, Dates, and Statistics

This section provides for the parent the following documents, forms, samples, and/or blank pages for recording personal information about each child:

1. State and Local Homeschooling Requirements
2. Yearly Calendar
3. Health Records
4. Appointments
5. Field Trips, Special Activities
6. Achievements, Awards
7. High School Transcript Form — incomplete and complete (in appendix)
8. Sample Affidavit — a requirement in some states expressing parents' intent (in appendix)

State and Local Homeschooling Requirements

_____

_____

_____

_____

_____

_____

_____

_____

_____

_____

_____

_____

_____

_____

_____

_____

_____

_____

_____

_____

_____

_____

_____

_____

Yearly Calendar

116

Health Records

_____

_____

_____

_____

_____

_____

_____

_____

_____

_____

_____

_____

_____

_____

_____

_____

_____

_____

_____

_____

_____

_____

Appointments

Field Trips, Special Activities

_____

_____

_____

_____

_____

_____

_____

_____

_____

_____

_____

_____

_____

_____

_____

_____

_____

_____

_____

_____

_____

_____

_____

_____

_____

_____

_____

Achievements, Awards

Notes

_____

_____

_____

_____

_____

_____

_____

_____

_____

_____

_____

_____

_____

_____

_____

_____

_____

_____

_____

_____

_____

_____

_____

_____

_____

Appendix

SAMPLE*

Transcript of High School Record

NAME: Susan C. Blue   DATE OF BIRTH: 8/29/87
ADDRESS: 1750 Washy Rd.   CITY: Middleburg
ENTRANCE DATE: Fall 2002   GRAD. DATE: Spring 2006

	FRESHMAN YEAR 2002–2003			SOPHOMORE YEAR 2003–2004		
	COURSE TITLE	Gr.	Cr.	COURSE TITLE	Gr.	Cr.
ENGLISH (4 years Req)	**Eng. 9**	**B**	**1**	**Eng.10**	**A**	**1**
MATH (3 years Req)	**Alg. 1**	**B**	**1**	**Alg. 2**	**B**	**.5**
SCIENCE (3 years Req)	**Biol.**	**B**	**1**	**Phys. Sci.**	**B**	**1**
SOC. ST. (3 years Req)	**Hist. of Civ.**	**C**	**1**	**W. History**	**A**	**1**
ARTS & HUMAN. (2 years Req)	**Music**	**B**	**1**	**Art**	**B**	**.5**
	German	**P**	**.5**	**German**	**P**	**.5**
				Home Ec.	**A**	**1**
OTHER	**Health**	**B**	**.5**			
	P.E.	**P**	**.25**	**P.E.**	**S**	**.5**

Gr. = Grade: A= Excellent, B = Good, C = Fair, D = Poor, P = Pass,
   G = Good, S = Satisfactory
Cr. is Credit: Unit of credit is years. 1 = 1 year, .5 = ½ year, .25 = ¼ year

*This transcript form may be reproduced for student use.

Home Education Program

SOC. SEC. # 000-00-0000
STATE: PA   ZIP: 17842
COURSE: ACADEMIC

JUNIOR YEAR 2004–2005			SENIOR YEAR 2005–2006		
COURSE TITLE	Gr.	Cr.	COURSE TITLE	Gr.	Cr.
Eng.11	**B**	**1**	**Eng.12**	**B**	**1**
Alg. 2	**C**	**.5**	**Consum.**	**B**	**1**
Chem.	**B**	**1**			
U.S.Hist.	**B**	**1**			
			Home Ec.	**B**	**.5**
P.E.	**S**	**.5**	**P.E.**	**G**	**1**

EVALUATOR'S SIGNATURE: _____
Or other required signatures

SIGNATURE OF HOMESCHOOL SUPERVISOR _____

Transcript of High School Record

NAME: **DATE OF BIRTH:**
ADDRESS: **CITY:**
ENTRANCE DATE: **GRAD. DATE:**

FRESHMAN YEAR 20___–20___			SOPHOMORE YEAR 20___–20___		
COURSE TITLE	Gr.	Cr.	COURSE TITLE	Gr.	Cr.

ENGLISH
(4 years Req)

MATH
(3 years Req)

SCIENCE
(3 years Req)

SOC. ST.
(3 years Req)

ARTS &
HUMAN.
(2 years Req)
OTHER

Gr. = Grade: A= Excellent, B = Good, C = Fair, D = Poor, P = Pass,
G = Good, S = Satisfactory
Cr. is Credit: Unit of credit is years. 1 = 1 year, .5 = ½ year, .25 = ¼ year

This transcript form may be reproduced for student use.

Home Education Program

SOC. SEC. #
STATE: **ZIP: 17842**
COURSE:

JUNIOR YEAR   **SENIOR YEAR**
20____–20____   20____–20____

COURSE TITLE Gr. Cr.   COURSE TITLE   Gr.   Cr.

EVALUATOR'S SIGNATURE: _____

Or other required signatures

SIGNATURE OF HOMESCHOOL SUPERVISOR _____

Sample of PA State Required Affidavit

(to be completed, notarized, and submitted to the local school district at the beginning of every school year.)

AFFIDAVIT OF THE SUPERVISIOR OF A HOME EDUCATION PROGRAM

The compulsory education section of the Pennyslvania school code states:

It is the policy of the Commonwealth to preserve the primary right of the parent or parents, or person or persons in loco parentis to a child, to choose the education and training for each child.

COMMONWEALTH OF PENNSYLVANIA
COUNTY OF _____
SS:
Before me the undersigned notary public, this day personally appeared
_____ , being first duly sworn on oath, deposes and says:

I attest that I am a parent or guardian or other person having legal custody of the child or children listed below, that I am responsible for the provision of instruction in his/her/their home education program in which the following courses are offered in the English language for a minimum of nine hundred (900) hours of instruction at the elementary school level or nine hundred ninety (990) hours of instruction at the secondary school level, and that the home education program is otherwise in compliance with the provisions of the Public School Code:

At the ELEMENTARY SCHOOL LEVEL the following courses shall be taught: English, to include spelling, reading, and writing; arithmetic; science; geography; history of the United States and Pennsylvania; civics; safety education, including regular and continuous instruction in the dangers and prevention of fires; health and physiology; physical education; music; and art.

At the SECONDARY SCHOOL LEVEL the following courses shall be taught: English, to include language, literature, speech and composition; science; geography; social studies, to include civics, world history, history of the United States and Pennsylvania; mathematics, to include general mathematics, algebra, and geometry; art; music; physical education; health and safety education, including regular and continuous instruction in the dangers and prevention of fires. Other courses may be included at the discretion of the supervisor.

I also attest that each child in the home education program has received the health and medical services required by Article XIV of the Public School Code and that a comprehensive health record is being maintained for each child. I also attest that I have a high school diploma or its equivalent, and that all adults living in the home and education program have not been convicted, within five years immediately preceding the date of the affidavit, of the criminal offenses enumerated in subsection (E) of section 111 of the school code. These offenses relate to criminal homicide, aggravated assault, kidnapping, unlawful restraint, rape, statutory rape, involuntary deviate sexual intercourse, indecent assault, indecent exposure, concealing a death of child born out of wedlock, endangering welfare of children, dealing in infant children, corruption of minors, and sexual abuse of children. They also include felony offenses relating to prostitution and related offenses, and felony offenses relating to obscene and other sexual materials.

Attached is:

1. An outline of proposed education objectives by subject area.

2. Evidence that each child has been immunized or has a religious or medical exemption from immunizations.

3. Evidence of supervisor's graduation from High School or College or attainment of a General Equivalency Diploma (GED).

4. If a child in the home education program has been identified pursuant to the provisions of the education of the handicapped act of needing special education services, excluding those students identified as gifted or talented, then also attached is written notification of approval from a Pennsylvania-certified special education teacher, or a licensed clincial psychologist, or a certified school psychologist that this program addresses the specific needs of the student.

Name of Supervisor of Home Education Program _____

Address of Home Education Program Site   _____

City _____ State ____ Zip ___ County _____

Phone number of home education program site _____

Name and age of each child who shall participate in the program:

_____

_____

_____

Signature _____

Subscribed and sworn before me this day _____ (date)

File with Superintendent School District of Resident prior to commencement of the Home Education Program and annually thereafter on August 1st.

NOTARIZATION:

Notary Public _____

Compliments of Dr. Howard Richman, Pennsylvania Homeschoolers Accreditation Agency, Kittanning, PA.

Index

Notes

Notes

Notes

Notes

Notes

Notes

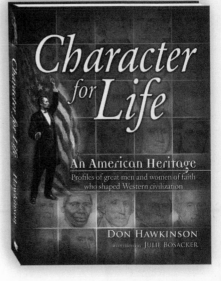
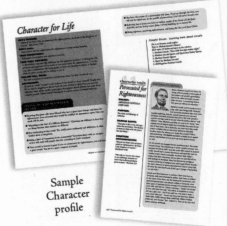

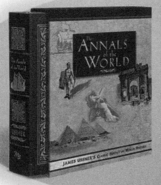